FOLK TOYS

FOLK TOYS

Compiled by Li Youyou

 FOREIGN LANGUAGES PRESS

First Edition 2008

ISBN 978-7-119-04674-7

©Foreign Languages Press, Beijing, China, 2008

Published by

Foreign Languages Press

24 Baiwanzhuang Road, Beijing 100037, China

http: //www. flp. com. cn

Distributed by

China International Book Trading Corporation

35 Chegongzhuang Xilu, Beijing 100044, China

P.O. Box 399, Beijing, China

Printed in the People's Republic of China

Contents

Autumn / 75

Winter / 105

INTRODUCTION

Chinese folk toys, derived from games, work, religious and shamanistic activities and folk customs, are as old as the people themselves are. There is a wide variety of types of such toys in China. Drawing on local resources, these well-designed and bright-colored toys are practical as well as decorative works of art.

History

The origin of Chinese folk toys could date back to primitive society. Many elaborate stone and ceramic balls of different sizes were found among the excavations at the Banpo site of the Yangshao Neolithic culture (4800-4300 BC), unearthed in 1958 in Xi'an. The archeologists believed these to be playthings for children at the time. Among the funerary objects excavated in this site from the grave of a girl, about five to six years old, people found 79 pieces of pottery, stone balls and beads, as well as bone earrings and beads. This has proved that, besides their hunting use, stone and ceramic balls were used as children's toys 6,000 years ago.

Ceramic and stone balls, excavated from Xi'an Banpo and Lintong Jiangzhai ruins

Dog, ceramic, Han Dynasty, from collection of Kong Lingxi

Ceramic *yun* (ancient musical instrument), excavated from Hemudu ruins, Zhejiang Province

Ox carriage, ceramic, Eastern Han Dynasty,
from collection of the Handan Museum

Foal, bronze, Western Zhou Dynasty,
from collection of the Henan Museum

Chicks, ceramic, Eastern Han Dynasty,
from collection of the Handan Museum

During the latter Shang Dynasty (1300-1046 BC), China's bronze smelting techniques reached its peak. From the Yin ruins at Xiaotun Village, Anyang City, Henan Province, people unearthed a 6cm-long and 4cm-wide bronze box cover, on which there were some inscriptions of characters meaning "the King ordered this toy made for the girl." The box and aforementioned toy were not found; however, this was able to prove that there had been toys made particularly for children in the Yin Dynasty.

During the Eastern Han Dynasty (25-220), toys developed rapidly and circulated in the markets. According to historical records, at that time, some people sold as children's toys items like earthen catapult balls, "earthen carriages and dogs," and figures riding horses or playing. Among the unearthed funerary objects of Eastern Han tombs, there are many ceramic and wooden figurines, ceramic pigs, dogs, chicken and other animals, as well as ceramic houses, granary, towers and wells, and so on. Those funerary objects could also be used as toys. A Han rock found in Nanyang, Henan Province was carved with three playing children, one child holds a wooden turtledove-shaped toy in his hand; another pulls a turtledove-shaped cart, and the third one behind it is posed whipping and driving the cart. This picture shows wooden toys had appeared during the Han Dynasty.

Vendor Selling Toys to Children,
Song Dynasty, painting by Li Song

Between the Sui and Tang dynasties (581-907), the appearance of colored ceramic works like Tang Tricolor directly influenced the manufacture of toys. Earthen and ceramic toys improved greatly in material and color. Porcelain toys began to appear too. The Shaanxi Museum has collected many small ceramic toys including chicks, dogs, figures and winnowing pans, excavated from Sui's "Tomb of a Child Named Li." In September 1973, in the Tang-dynasty Astana ancient tombs in Tur-

Five frolicking children, clay, Song Dynasty,
from collection of the Zhenjiang Museum

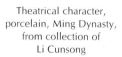
Theatrical character,
porcelain, Ming Dynasty,
from collection of
Li Cunsong

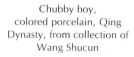
Chubby boy,
colored porcelain, Qing
Dynasty, from collection of
Wang Shucun

Chubby boy,
porcelain, Song Dynasty,
from collection of
Wang Shucun

pan, Xinjiang, a group of four women earthen figurines was unearthed: one is turning a millstone to grind rice into flour; one is making pastry; one is husking rice with a mortar and pestle; and the last is choosing and picking through some grains in winnowing pans. These earthen figurines, with color painted on their heads and clothes, are proportionally shaped, looking lifelike. Their vivid expressions and postures show us an interesting working scene.

In the Song Dynasty (960-1279), traditional Chinese toys entered their most prosperous stage. Commerce became relatively developed during this period, and the cultural life of citizens evolved rapidly. Toys became a part of citizens' daily life. There were various kinds of toys, including clay, ceramic, wooden and bamboo toys, among which clay toys were the most popular. From the Wutiaojie Song ruins at Zhenjiang, a set of five children figurines was discovered. Climbing, lying down, standing or sitting, these children have different postures and vivid expressions. This figure group is very valuable since it exhibits the earthen sculpture skill level in China during the Song Dynasty. From the time of the Song, the production and sales of earthen toys became an industry all over China.

Human-mask whistle, Tang Tricolor, Tang Dynasty, from collection of Li Cunsong

In the Ming and Qing period (1368-1911), both the commercialization and specialization of traditional toys made new progress. Special shops and professional handicraft workshops for toys emerged, and toy production bases with different local characteristics appeared. The toys were made out of various materials including clay, ceramic, wood and bamboo, paper and straw. In folk custom activities, toys also became indispensable.

In the early 20th century, folk toys reached a zenith. Mechanical iron toys were batch-produced. In the middle and late 20th century, in order to assist and support the folk toy industry, the Chinese government transformed many famous handicraft workshops into research institutes and modern workshops, such as the

Practical toy, food,
Weixian County,
Hebei Province

Big Afu, clay, Qing Dynasty,
from collection of Wuxi
Huishan Clay Figure Research
Institute

Sound toy, ceramic whistle,
Jianshui, Yunnan Province

Ornamental toy, Tianjin Zhang
Clay Figurine Master Workshop,
made by Yang Zhizhong

Wooden toys, Zhejiang

Wuxi Huishan Clay Figure Research Institute and the Tianjin Zhang Clay Figurine Master Workshop. But over time, plastic, plush, mechanical and electric toys have gradually replaced the various traditional toys.

Classification of Toys

Chinese folk toys can be found across the country. Most of them are made out of local materials, therefore they have observable local characteristics. The various kinds of toys are divided into the following categories, according to their functions:

Spring toy, kite with the design of "Five Bats Encircling a Peach" (Peach is symbolic of longevity), made by Li Guokun, Beijing

1. Seasonal toys

Seasonal toys, closely connected with folk custom activities, are always timely. For example, pinwheels in temple fairs during the Chinese New Year (or Spring Festival); colorful lanterns with puzzles for the Yuanxiao Festival (15th of 1st lunar month); small cloth sachets filled with fragrant herbal powder (fragrant sachet) in the shape of tigers for warding off evil spirits and poisonous things during the Dragon-boat Festival (5th of 5th lunar month); Mr. Rabbit for the Mid-Autumn Festival (15th of 8th lunar month); and clay hanging tigers, roaring tigers and lions (tiger- or lion-shaped clay whistles) for warding off evil spirits, and toy tigers for Lunar New Year's Eve.

Seasonal toy, Beijing kite, made by Zheng Jun

Introduction

2. Ornamental toys

This category often relates to legends and fairytales, for bringing good fortune and keeping away evil spirits. Ornamental toys such as clay tigers standing at house corners and hanging fragrant sachets are people's favorites.

3. Sound toys

Children especially like these toys, since they are amusing and exciting. They include mainly ceramic toys, porcelain and clay whistles, rattle-drums, small gongs and drums, and sound carts.

4. Practical toys

Practical toys are things that can also be used as bedding or even food. Tiger pillows and ear pillows, sugar dolls and dough figurines are some examples.

5. Aptitude toys

The main function of this category is to develop children's intelligence and improve their brain activity by combining both logic and amusement. Examples include the seven-piece jigsaw puzzle, puzzle rings, and Kongming lock puzzle.

Bamboo, wooden and clay toy boat, Guangxi Zhuang Autonomous Region

Cloth toy, fragrant sachet, Shaanxi Province

Woven and ceramic toys, Hubei Province

Spring toy, clay, produced in Fengxiang, Shaanxi

Spring toys, clay figurine whistles, Junxian County, Henan Province

Spring toy, clay, Huaiyin, Henan

In terms of materials, Chinese folk toys can also be classified into clay, ceramic, wooden, bamboo, cloth, woven straw, paper, food and stone toys.

China's traditional festivals are many, signified by the expression of "four seasons and eight festivals." The four seasons are spring, summer, autumn and winter. The eight festivals are Spring Festival (China's most ceremonious festival on 1st day of 1st lunar month), Yuanxiao Festival (15th of 1st lunar month, as the first full-moon night of the lunar year, a continuation of spring celebrations), Qingming Festival (people sweep tombs and make ritual offerings to ancestors on this traditional day), Duanwu or Dragon-boat Festival (people eat *zongzi*, pyramid-shaped dumpling made of glutinous rice wrapped in bamboo or reed leaves, and race dragon-boats, on 5th day of 5th lunar month), Zhongyuan Festival (a Taoist festival on 15th of 7th lunar month), Zhongqiu or Mid-Autumn Festival (all Chinese families are reunited on this important festival, on 15th of 8th lunar month), Dongzhi or Midwinter Day (between 22nd to 23rd every December, was fixed earliest among the 24 seasonal division points) and Chuxi (Lunar New Year's Eve, last day

Summer toy, cloth tiger,
Beijing

Winter toy, Nezha dough figurine,
Guanxian County, Shandong
Province

Spring toy, roly-poly,
Yutian, Hebei

Winter toy, clay hanging
tiger, Shaanxi

Summer toy, fragrant sachet,
Shaanxi

Winter toy, large
clay tiger, Fengxiang,
Shaanxi

Winter toys, Beijing, made by
Shuang Qixiang, Beijing

Autumn toy, Mr.
Rabbit, made by Shuang
Qixiang, Beijing

Opera story, engraved
calabashes, Gansu Province

of the lunar year). All these festivals are closely related
with agriculture, religion, and national and folk customs.
Chinese folk toys have always been connected with legends
and literary quotations around these festivals. They are
representatives of the content of the festivals. This is their
most outstanding feature.

Spring toys, made by Ma Yulan, Tianjin Zhang Clay
Figurine Master Workshop

Folk artisan Shuang Qixiang, with his clay toys

SPRING

Spring winds blow, pinwheels spin.
Fine days in the first four seasonal division points foretell
the harvest year.

Spring

Big Afu

"Big Afu," whose image is a healthy chubby boy, is representative of clay babies. Always smiling and wearing a brocade robe, this chubby boy always with a green lion in its arms is very lovely. A folk legend tells us, in ancient times, people in the Hui-shan area, Wuxi, Jiangsu, suffered so much from venomous snakes and ferocious beasts. Later, Heaven sent a child called "Shahai'er" to this area to save the people. The little boy was capable. When he smiled, the venomous snakes and ferocious beasts did not dare move. Therefore, he could easily kill and eat them. He ended the calamity and saved all people there. To commemorate this little boy, people made colored clay figurines of him, called "Afu," to bring fortune and keep away evil spirits.

Big Afu, clay, made by Yu Xianglian and Wang Nanxian, Wuxi, Jiangsu

Fuwa, clay, made by Shuang
Qixiang, Beijing

Fuwa, clay, made by Shuang
Qixiang, Beijing

Figurine of a child holding a green lion, clay, made by Li Huiyu and Ding Zhongfang, Wuxi, Jiangsu

Figurine of a child holding two monkeys, clay, made by Shuang Qixiang, Beijing

Figurines of a child bringing fortune, clay,
made by Shuang Yan, Beijing

Figurines of a child presenting flowers, clay,
made by Shuang Qixiang, Beijing

Abundant Every Year

This is a figurine of a child holding a fish in its arms. Since in Chinese, "fish" (*yu*) is the homophone of "abundance" (*yu*), this figurine signifies an abundant and flourishing life every year. People believe that putting such a figurine in one's home during the Spring Festival will bring good fortune for the whole year.

Abundant every year, clay, Niejiazhuang Village, Gaomi, Shandong

Figurines of a child holding a large carp ("*li*"), homophone of profit ("*li*"), clay, made by Shuang Qixiang, Beijing

Abundant every year, made by Yang Zhizhong, Tianjin Zhang Clay
Figurine Master Workshop

Little Boy of Wealth

The figurine image comprises a boy, silver and gold ingots and copper coins, indicating a rich and flourishing family.

Little boy of wealth, clay, Wuxi, Jiangsu, made by Li Huiyu and Ding Zhongfang

Figurine of a child holding a peach, clay, Huimin, Shandong

Figurine of a child sitting on a rock, clay, Dangchang, Gansu

Roly-poly

The roly-poly's special center of gravity keeps it standing, no matter how people push it. Its images are always chubby kids, old men or clown officials. Children are very fond of it.

Girl roly-polys, Yutian, Hebei

Kite

China is the birthplace of the kite. Kites are not only a famous type of Chinese craftwork but also traditional toys. When spring comes, with the pleasant spring breezes, people fly their good wishes along with the kites into the sky. The kite has a bamboo frame covered with paper or silk, painted with some colorful pictures. Riding on wind, a kite may go up higher and higher, while a string attached to it is held by a person. The designs of kites include flowers, birds, fish, insects, auspicious animals, figures and utensils.

Green lobster kite,
Weifang, Shandong

Catfish ("*nianyu*", homophone
of "abundant year") kite, made
by Fei Baoling, Beijing

"Enjoy Both Happiness and Longevity" kite, made by
Liu Hanxiang, Tianjin

Enjoy Both Happiness and Longevity

Bat represents happiness as it is a homophone of Chinese character
"*fu*", and peach is a symbol of longevity. So this kite, with those two
images, is called "Enjoy Both Happiness and Longevity".

Five Bats Flying around Chinese Character "Longevity"

The bat is an auspicious animal to the Chinese, as its pronunciation is similar to another character meaning happiness. This is a common design Chinese people use when celebrating one's birthday anniversary.

Five bats flying around Chinese character "longevity", made by Zhou Shutang, Tianjin

Kite with the design of five bats flying around a peach, symbol of longevity, made by Li Guokun, Beijing

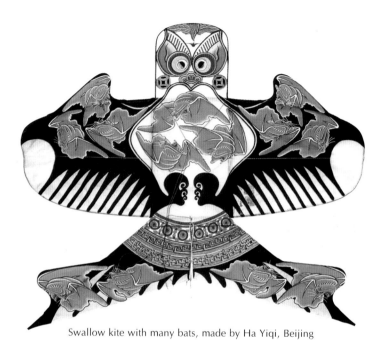

Swallow kite with many bats, made by Ha Yiqi, Beijing

Swallow Kite

This is one of the typical traditional Beijing kites. Its image is a swallow. When painting it, people always add some flowers, birds and insects on the swallow's wings, chest and tail.

Swallow kite with a design of goldfish, made by Liu Yongkuan, Beijing

Cicada kite, Weifang, Shandong

Sun Wukong (Monkey King from *Journey to the West*) kite, Weifang, Shandong

Butterfly kite, Tianjin, made by Wei Shuichang

Spring Ox

The ox is a symbol of industriousness and honesty. It is also considered as an auspicious creature bringing harvests and keeping away floods. Several days before the Beginning of Spring (in February, one of the 24 seasonal division points), people piled soil into the shape of an ox. At dawn of the day of the Beginning of Spring, officials led the masses to march around it and hold the ceremony called "Beating the Spring Ox," symbolizing the start of farming. Folk artisans made clay spring oxen for sale in the market. People bought them as gifts, and children played with them. This expressed people's good wishes for the harvest.

Spring ox, cloth, Licheng, Shanxi Province

Buffalo, clay, Huaiyang, Henan

Little cowherd and his cow, clay, Niejiazhuang Village,
Gaomi, Shandong

Spring toy, clay, Fengxiang, Shaanxi

Buffalo, ceramic whistle, Yazhou,
Guizhou Province

Buffalo, ceramic whistle,
Jianshui, Yunnan

Buffalo, ceramic whistle, Yazhou, Guizhou

Ox, clay whistle, Junxian County, Henan

Buffalo, ceramic whistle, Yazhou, Guizhou

Cat Guarding Silkworms

The sericulture industry was developed in the areas south of the lower reaches of the Yangtze River. In ancient times, an important task to protect silkworms was preventing damage from mice. One method was putting a colored clay cat beside the silkworms' beds to scare away mice. These scary and sturdy clay cats came in different sizes. The small ones were also children's toys.

Cats guarding silkworms, clay, Wuxi, Jiangsu

Cat guarding silkworms, clay, Wuxi, Jiangsu, and Jiaxing, Zhejiang

Black cat, hanging fragrant sachet,
Fengxiang, Shaanxi

Cat, clay, Linyi, Shandong

Cat, hanging fragrant sachet, Xi'an, Shaanxi

Clay Whistles of Junxian County

Junxian County of Henan has a rich variety of clay toys. Many of them are whistles. In old days, women from rural areas used to buy clay whistles from temple fairs, and on their way home, they would throw them to the children along the road. This was a way to pray for boy babies.

A pair of lions, clay whistles, Junxian County, Henan

Lions with bushy manes, clay whistles, Junxian County, Henan

Twelve animals (symbolizing the year a person is born in), clay whistle, made by Wang Lantian, Junxian County, Henan

Monkey group, clay whistles, Junxian County, Henan

Horses, clay whistles, Junxian County, Henan

Ninigou

Huaiyang's *ninigou* is a kind of clay toy with colorful paintings on its black surface sold at temple fairs. People believed it could keep away evil spirits, and bring good fortune as well as sons. These colorful sculptures are always simple, unsophisticated yet mysteriously appealing. For example, there is one that looks like a monkey but with a human face, and also dogs, fish, tortoises, wild geese, as well as imaginary strange birds and beasts.

Monster, *ninigou*, Huaiyang, Henan

Spring

Unicorn, *ninigou*, Huaiyang, Henan

Monster, *ninigou*, Huaiyang, Henan

Renzu monkey, *ninigou*,
Huaiyang, Henan

Renzu Monkey

Renzu monkey is a representative work of *ninigou* produced in Huai-yang, Henan. It features designs symbolizing female genitals, representing sexual-organ worship of primitive humans.

Facial Makeup on Small Ladles

During the Chinese New Year in ancient times, people used to celebrate by way of parading in streets, which was called "*Shehuo*". On the occasion, along with people's favorite dragon dances and lion dances, there were also performers on horses wearing stage costumes and donning masks or facial makeup, performing operettas and dances to exorcise evil ghosts. Later, such facial makeup came to be drawn on wooden ladles for feeding horses. The larger ones were hung in courtyards for decoration or repelling epidemic spirits, while the smaller ones were carried by children as playthings.

Theatrical character on small ladle, wood, Baoji, made by Li Jiyou, Shaanxi

Facial makeup on small ladle, wood, made by Li Jiyou, Baoji, Shaanxi

Beijing Opera Masks

Spearhead, wood,
Tancheng, Shandong

Shadow-play character, wood,
Fengxiang, Shaanxi

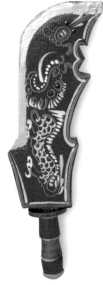

Large sword, wood,
Tancheng, Shandong

These are playthings for children.

Monk Xuanzang and his disciples (characters from
the classic novel *Journey to the West*), clay mask,
made by Ren Yude, Weixian County, Hebei

Silang Visits His Mother

In the early 10th century, troops of the Song and Liao dynasties were pitted against each other. The king of the Liao invited Emperor Taizong of the Song to a banquet with the intention of killing him. Yang Linggong learned of this trap, and ordered his eldest son to disguise as Emperor Taizong and attend the banquet in Prefecture Youzhou with his other sons. At the banquet, a fight occurred, and his fourth son Yang Yanhui, normally known as Silang, was captured. Fifeen years later, the war between the Song and the Liao broke out again. The wife of Yang Linggong led the Song troops. Silang, who had married a princess of the Liao Dynasty, had been missing his mother very much. His wife, the princess, on learning of this, helped him go to the Song troops' camp to visit his mother.

Silang Visits His Mother, clay, made by Han Zengqi, Beijing

Drama story, clay, made by Han Zengqi, Beijing

Bristle Figures

Bristle figures are a unique toy of Beijing, with a history of about a hundred years. The figure is generally about 10 cm high. People knead clay to make the figure's head and base, and use straw to make the frame of body. The inside is filled with cotton and the outside is covered with colored paper or silk. With facial makeup and opera costume drawn on, a bristle figure is completed. When people fix some springy bristles on a figure's base, the figure, placed in a bronze plate, will automatically move with the vibrations from beating of the plate.

Bristle figures from drama story, made by Bai Dacheng, Beijing

SUMMER

Fifth day of the fifth lunar month is the
Duanwu (Dragon-boat) Festival,
The cloth tiger will repel the "Five Poisonous Creatures."

Summer

Tiger-shaped Cloth Fragrant Sachets Filled with Moxa and Spice

Ancient Chinese believed that tigers could repel evil things, so many worshiped the tiger. On the occasion of the Duanwu (Dragon-boat) Festival, people used to wear tiger-shaped cloth fragrant sachets filled with moxa and spice. They were also used as children's toy.

Large tiger, cloth, Dazhai, Shanxi

Black tiger, cloth, Linfen, Shanxi

Tiger, cloth, Licheng, Shanxi

Tiger with a fish tail, cloth, Xinjiang, Shanxi

Tiger-shaped Pillow

This type of pillow is shaped like a tiger, and filled with cotton, buckwheat or paddy husks. The design of tiger heads is different from place to place. The production methods also slightly differ. Some are embroidered with colored threads; some made with colorful cloth; and others are drawn or pasted with colored paper. They were children's pillows as well as toys.

White-head tiger, cloth, Shanxi

Large-head tiger, cloth, Hebei

Little tigers, cloth, Weifang, Shandong

Little tigers, cloth, Beijing

Tiger-shaped pillow, cloth, Henan　　　　Tiger-shaped pillow, cloth, Hebei

Fragrant Sachet

Such sachets are filled with powder made from medicinal herbs that emit pleasant fragrances. For centuries, people of Han, Manchu, Mongol, Tujia and other ethnic groups all had the habit of wearing such sachets, especially during the Duanwu (Dragon-boat) Festival, believing they could keep away evils and disaster.

Two donkeys carrying a sedan-chair, hanging fragrant sachet,
Qingyang, Gansu

Horse, fragrant sachet, Qianyang, Shaanxi,
from collection of Zhang Jingjuan

Chinese dragon, fragrant sachet,
Qingyang, Gansu

Knot of eternity (representing
unending love and harmony), fragrant
sachet, Xi'an, Shaanxi

Butterfly, fragrant sachet, Xi'an, Shaanxi

Goose, fragrant sachet,
Qianyang, Shaanxi, from collection
of Zhang Jingjuan

Summer

Continuously Giving Birth to Sons

This hanging decoration comprised baby with a chubby face, lotus flowers and seedpods, a bamboo *sheng* (wind instrument, homophone meaning "to give birth"), carp (bearing quantities of roe), and so on. In Chinese, "lotus" (*lian*) sounds the same as "continuously." The design of a child growing from a lotus flower implies continuity of family. Lotus is also a favorite Chinese flower. Besides, it is a symbol of Buddhism.

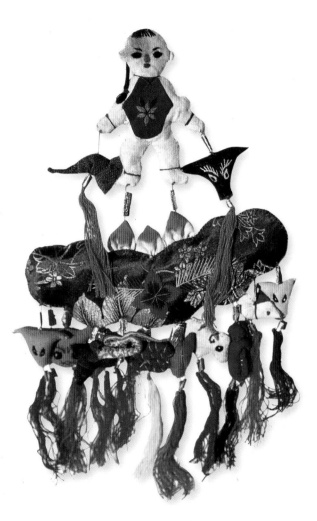

Continuously giving birth to sons,
hanging fragrant sachet, Qingyang, Gansu

Doll with three faces, hanging fragrant sachet,
Qingyang, Gansu

Fish Doll

Fish have long been considered auspicious by Chinese people, endowed with much symbolism. "Fish" (*yu*) is the homophone of "abundant," therefore signifying a life of abundance; and the carp, bearing large quantities of roe, symbolizes fertility and flourishing families. Combining fish with a doll expresses people's good wishes for a flourishing family and abundant life.

Fish doll, hanging fragrant sachet, Qingyang, Gansu

58

Fish doll, hanging fragrant sachet, Qingyang, Gansu

Fish doll, hanging fragrant sachet, Qingyang, Gansu

Doll with Two Twisted Knots of Hair

The doll-shaped fragrant sachet has on its head a pair of symmetrical knots of hair designed like chicks. On the arms, shoulders and clothes, there are often such symmetrical chick or rabbit decorative designs.

Doll with two twisted knots of hair, hanging fragrant sachet, Luochuan, Shaanxi

Crab-shaped Hanging Fragrant Sachet

Fragrant sachets of crab design also have the function of keeping away evil spirits and disasters.

Crab forming the character *"Shou"* (longevity), hanging
fragrant sachet, Qingyang, Gansu

Crab with "Five Poisons," hanging fragrant sachet, Qingyang, Gansu,
from collection of Zeng Jie

"Five Poisons"

Ancient Chinese generally called the scorpion, centipede, snake, lizard and toad, the "Five Poisons." Children's clothes and fragrant sachets were embroidered with the "Five Poisonous" creatures to combat evil spirits with their venomous powers.

Five poisonous creatures, hanging decoration, clay, Fengxiang, Shaanxi

Frog Design Pillow with "Five Poisons"

The frog is of the same family as the toad in the "Five Poisons." In the center of the pillow, there is a hole as large as a cup into which a child can comfortably tuck his ear when sleeping. This pillow was also made for keeping away evil spirits and disaster from children.

Frog design pillow with "Five Poisons," cloth, Qianyang, Shaanxi, from collection of Liu Yakun

Frog design pillow with the "Five Poisons," cloth, Qianyang, Shaanxi

Clay Mold

Piggy Zhu Bajie (character from *Journey to the West*), clay mold, Xincheng, Hebei

Goose with flower in its mouth, clay mold, Xincheng, Hebei

Feeding cow, clay mold, Xincheng, Hebei

Theatric characters, clay mold, Xincheng, Hebei

Theatrical character, clay mold, Xincheng, Hebei

Theatrical character, clay mold, Xincheng, Hebei

Engraved Calabash

Because calabash is pronounced "*hulu*," sounding like "*fu*" and "*lu*," which mean happiness and wealth and rank. It was beloved by all Chinese as an auspicious sign. Calabash can produce many seeds, and its vine ("*mandai*") is very similar in pronunciation to "*wandai*" (ten thousand generations), so it also suggests that a family will have endless offspring. The themes of engravings on calabash include historical tales, legends, fairytales, opera stories, and auspicious designs. Through processes like peeling, dyeing, engraving and varnishing, a calabash becomes a finished product.

Engraved calabashes, Gansu

Calabash carved with the design of katydid, Liaocheng, Shandong

Engraved calabash, Gansu

Jingling Bamboo Basket

This is a sound toy. Before the small basket, which is weaved with dyed bamboo strips, takes its final shape, people would put some small triangular iron pieces into it. When shaken, the iron pieces will jingle. This interesting toy can easily attract a baby's attention.

Jingling bamboo baskets, Shandong

Bamboo baskets, Sichuan and Zhejiang

Water wagon, bamboo and wood, Jiangsu

Bamboo chairs, Jiangsu

Braided Grass Creatures

It is quite common throughout China to use fibrous grasses to weave various animals and hanging decorations. Children are very fond of such lively grass insects, dragons and phoenixes, and twelve zodiac animals, braided by skilled folk artisans.

Crabs, braided grass, made by
Yuyong Aisin Gioro, Beijing

Tortoises, braided grass, made by
Yuyong Aisin Gioro, Beijing

Shrimp, braided grass, made by
Yuyong Aisin Gioro, Beijing

Grasshoppers, braided grass, made by
Yuyong Aisin Gioro, Beijing

Crickets, braided grass, made by
Yuyong Aisin Gioro, Beijing

Chinese dragon woven with hemp, Guizhou

Birds woven with wheat straw

Decorated basket woven with wheat straw

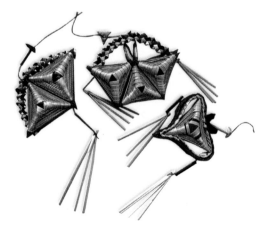

Hanging decorations woven with wheat straw

Horse woven with hemp, Guizhou

Horse woven with wheat straw

Huangping's Clay Whistle

Huangping's clay whistle is a toy of the Miao ethnic group. Its sculptures often imitate the animals living in Miao mountainous areas, instilled with strong local characteristics. The whistle should first be kneaded out of clay; then all kinds of ornamental patterns are printed on it by tools; after it has taken shape, it is dried in the shade; then fired, before it is painted with bright colors; and finally it is covered with egg white or polish oil.

Dragonfly fired clay whistles, made by Wu Guoqing (Miao ethnic group), Huangping, Guizhou

Lyrebird fired clay whistles, made by Wu Guoqing, Huangping, Guizhou

Monkey fired clay whistles, made by Wu Guoqing,
Huangping, Guizhou

Rhinoceros fired clay whistle,
made by Wu Guoqing, Huangping,
Guizhou

Snake fired clay whistle, from
collection of Lan Xianlin (Miao
ethnic group), Huangping, Guizhou

Tiger fired clay whistle, from collection
of Lan Xianlin, Huangping, Guizhou

Tijiang Dough Figurines

Tijiang Dough Figurines are pastries with stuffing. The prepared stuffing is put into the kneaded paste, which is then shaped into figures in different molds, and finally baked in an oven. People present this pastry to children, with wishes that they grow up healthy and safe.

Bodhisattva Guanyin, Tijiang dough figurine, Weixian County, Hebei

God of Longevity, Tijiang dough figurine, Weixian County, Hebei

AUTUMN

The moon is full on the 15th of the 8th lunar month,
Families are reuniting, and Mr. Rabbit is smiling.

Autumn

Mr. Rabbit

Mr. Rabbit is a seasonal toy popular in Beijing. Legend tells us that, on the moon is found not only the Goddess of Moon, Chang'e, but also a jade rabbit, which can produce medicines curing all illnesses. So, on every Mid-Autumn Festival on the 15th of the eighth lunar month, people will make offerings to Mr. Rabbit (clay). The image of Mr. Rabbit has a rabbit head but a human body. It carries a pestle, and wears armor and a red gown. Some ride a tiger, deer, qilin (Chinese kylin), while others sit on lotus flowers or other flower seats with cloud patterns. This is an auspicious decoration for the festival, as well as being a folk toy popular among children.

A mountain of "Mr. Rabbits" for sale, Temple of the God of Eastern Sacred Mountain, Beijing

Big Mr. Rabbit, clay, made by Bai
Dacheng and Ren Yude, Beijing

Mr. Rabbit, clay, made by Shuang Qixiang, Beijing

Mr. Rabbit, clay, made by Shuang Qixiang, Beijing

Rabbit King

There is a legend about how one year many adults and children fell sick in the Jinan area of Shandong. The Goddess of the Moon had the medicine for this illness, but refused to give it to poor people. Therefore, a poor man called Ren Han went to the moon on the 15th of the eighth lunar month to steal the medicine. He succeeded but could not find his way back. When the jade rabbit saw this, it took off its skin to cover Ren Han, who immediately turned to a jade rabbit and fled back to Jinan. Ren Han put the medicine into the spring in Jinan, and all the people were cured after drinking the water. To thank and commemorate the jade rabbit, people made a clay statue of it, and called it "Rabbit King."

Jade rabbit pounding medicine with a pestle, clay, made by Zhou Jingfu, Jinan, Shandong

Rabbit King, clay, made by Zhou Jingfu, Jinan, Shandong

Rabbit King, clay, made by Zhou Jingfu, Jinan, Shandong

Eight Immortals

In Chinese myth, there are eight legendary immortals. They are Han Zhongli who holds a palm-fan in hand, Zhang Guolao carrying a fisherman's drum, Han Xiangzi playing music on his jade *xiao* (vertical flute), Li Tieguai who carries a treasure calabash, Cao Guojiu who has in his palm a jade tablet, Lü Dongbin carrying a sword, Lan Caihe with a flower basket in hand, and He Xiangu holding a lotus flower. They once were trying to cross the sea, using the powers of the magic articles they were carrying. The united Eight Immortals ultimately crossed the sea successfully.

Eight Immortals, clay, Fengxiang, Shaanxi

Monkey Sun Wukong and Pig Zhu Bajie (characters from *Journey to the West*), clay, made by Han Zengqi, Beijing

Qilin (Chinese kylin) Bringing Sons

Qilin is a sacred animal in Chinese legend.
Common Chinese people believed that the
qilin could bring people sons.

Qilin bringing sons, clay, Fengxiang, Shaanxi

Boy on a lion entering the house,
clay, from collection of Lan Xianlin,
Niejiazhuang Village, Gaomi, Shandong

Immortal Zhang

Immortal Zhang has long been vener-
ated by the people for protecting newborn babies. It was believed that the
reason newborn babies died was that
an evil dog from the heavens hurt them.
Immortal Zhang was able to shoot down
the dog hiding in the clouds by using
his bow and arrows, and thus blessed
the babies. It is also said that Immortal
Zhang can bring sons.

Immortal Zhang on a cart, produced in the
Wuxi Clay Figurine Factory, Jiangsu

Pig Zhu Bajie (character from *Journey to the West*), *ninigou*, from collection of Wang Kangsheng, Huaiyang, Henan

Monkey Sun Wukong and Pig Zhu Bajie (characters from *Journey to the West*), clay whistle, Junxian County, Henan

Liu Bei, Guan Yu and Zhang Fei

These three figures are the major characters in the novel *Three Kingdoms*. They were sworn brothers who established the Kingdom of Shu.

Liu Bei, Guan Yu and Zhang Fei, clay, Cangshan, Shandong

Liu Bei, Guan Yu and Zhang Fei, clay, Fengxiang, Shaanxi

Legend of the White Snake

After a thousand years of cultivation, the White Snake finally became an immortal. She and her maid Qing'er (a green snake) came to the mortal world. When sightseeing at the West Lake, they encountered Xu Xian, who the White Snake fell in love with. Therefore, she summoned winds and rains, and borrowed an umbrella from Xu Xian, at which point their love story began.

Legend of the White Snake, clay, Fengxiang, Henan

Theatrical character,
princess, clay, Zhao'an,
Fujian

Zhuge Liang (character from
Three Kingdoms), clay,
Cangshan, Shandong

Autumn

Theatrical character,
clay, Shandong

Theatrical characters, clay, Wuxi, Jiangsu

Clay Whistles of Yuhuazhai Village

The sculptures of the black clay whistles produced in the village of Yuhuazhai, southern suburbs of Xi'an, are largely characters from local operas. The steps for making such a whistle are as follows: First, using local clay to make the sculpture by putting it in a mold, leaving a hole at the back. It is then fired and smoked until black; then colors are applied on it; and finally it is coated with egg white or polish oil. The succinct sculptures and distinct colors express strong local characteristics.

Theatrical character, clay whistle, Yuhuazhai Village, Xi'an

Theatrical character, clay whistle, Yuhuazhai Village, Xi'an

Theatrical character, clay whistle, Yuhuazhai Village, Xi'an

Liu Bei (character from
Three Kingdoms), clay whistle,
Yuhuazhai Village, Xi'an

Guang Yu (character from
Three Kingdoms), clay
whistle, Yuhuazhai
Village, Xi'an

Zhang Fei (character
from *Three Kingdoms*),
clay whistle, Yuhuazhai
Village, Xi'an

Old general Huang Zhong (character from
Three Kingdoms), clay, Yutian, Hebei

Theatrical character, clay, Yutian, Hebei

Animals

Roaring Lion

The lion symbolizes holiness and happiness in Buddhist tradition, and power in the mortal world. A lion-shaped toy was believed to bring good luck. The method to make a roaring lion toy is as follows: The front and the rear parts of the lion's body are made separately. After the parts are air-dried, they are connected with sheepskin or strong paper. With a small whistle placed inside its body, when the parts of the clay lion are pushed towards each other, the compressed air would make a sound through the open lion mouth.

Roaring lion, clay, Heilongjiang

Roaring lion, clay, Gansu

Roaring lion, clay, Leting, Hebei

Stone lion, Houma, Shanxi

Autumn

Sitting lion, clay, Fengxiang, Shaanxi

Green lion, clay, made by Wang
Tingting, Wuxi, Jiangsu

Lion Playing with a Colorful Ball

A lion is a fierce and majestic animal, so ancients believed that it could protect their houses from evil spirits. The colorful ball is also considered auspicious. The toy "lion playing with a colorful ball" is supposed to bring luck to people.

Lions playing with a colorful ball, cloth,
made by Hao Guijun, Weifang, Shandong

Chinese dragon, cloth, Qianyang, Shaanxi

Cloth lion, Henan, from collection
of Lan Xianlin

Bamboo Chinese dragon, Taishan, Shandong

Bamboo Chinese Dragons from Mount Tai

The bamboo Chinese dragon is a movable toy. The body of the dragon is made of bamboo sections, which are connected to each other with iron wires. The dragon's horns and claws are also made from bamboo branches through clipping or parching by fire. Designs are then carved or painted on the smoke-blackened dragon's head and body, and two red hemp balls are fixed on the head with springs. When a child holds its tail and shakes a little, the whole body of the bamboo dragon will twist left and right. A bamboo whistle is attached to its tail.

Sheep

In ancient China, the characters for sheep and auspiciousness were used without difference, so they always had the same meaning of "auspiciousness."

Sheep, cloth, Licheng, Shanxi

Sheep, clay, Fengxiang, Shaanxi

Clay Monkeys

Emotions like joy, anger and sadness along with movements of monkeys are vividly expressed in the clay monkey sculptures.

Naughty monkey, clay, made by Zhang Xihe, Junxian County, Henan

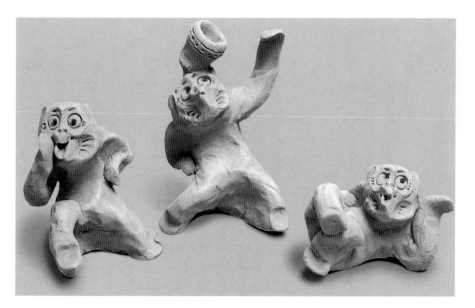

Monkeys, clay, made by Zhang Xihe, Junxian County, Henan

Stone Monkey from Fangcheng

The stone monkey represents a change of fate. The stone monkeys of Fangcheng, Henan, have many types.

"Conferred as Marquis Generation after Generation"

This phrase in Chinese is pronunced as "*bei bei feng hou*." People are fond of monkeys as they are clever and lively. In Chinese, "monkey" is pronounced "*hou*," the same as that of "marquis," while "back" sounds similar to "generation" (*bei*), and "*feng*" means "confer"; so the figurine of an old monkey carrying a young monkey on the back symbolizes being "conferred as marquis generation after generation."

Stone monkey,
Fangcheng, Henan

"Conferred as Marquis
Generation after Generation,"
clay, Hebei

"Conferred as Marquis Generation after
Generation," stone, Fangcheng, Henan

Clay monkeys, Huimin, Shandong

Hemp Monkeys

Hemp monkeys are a unique toy of Beijing. The toy's frame is made with two wires, covered with fluffy hemp dyed with colors. After tidying, a monkey toy is formed. As its main structure is wiry, it can be twisted at will to show the movements of monkeys.

Autumn

Hemp monkeys, Beijing

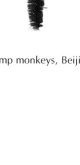

"Marriage of Mouse's Daughter"

"Marriage of Mouse's Daughter" is a popular folk story. A mouse wanted to seek a rich and powerful husband for his daughter. He went to the sun. The sun said, "I fear the cloud because it can cover me." So the mouse went to the cloud, which said, "I fear wind because it can blow me to bits." Then the mouse went to the wind, which said, "I fear the wall because it can block me." So the mouse went to the wall, which said, "I fear the mouse because it can burrow into me." In the end, the mouse thus found another mouse to be his daughter's husband.

"Marriage of Mouse's Daughter," clay sculpture, made by Liu Jilin, Beijing

Mice performing a wedding ceremony, clay sculpture, made by Liu Jilin, Beijing

Mouse bride, cloth, made by Hao Guijun, Weifang, Shandong

Rooster

The rooster can herald the break of the day, so the Chinese in the old days believed that the rooster was able to exorcise evil ghosts. In Chinese, "rooster" is pronounced "*ji*," similar to "luck," so images of the rooster are therefore called "lucky paintings." In China, there are various types of rooster toys made from materials like clay, cloth and ceramic.

Black cloth rooster, Longxian County, Shaanxi

Blue cloth rooster, Longxian County, Shaanxi

Roosters, clay sculpture, Yutian, Hebei

Autumn

Clay rooster whistles, Junxian County, Henan

Hawfinches, clay sculpture, Niejiazhuang Village,
Gaomi, Shandong

WINTER

Lunar New Year's Eve dinner, gifts of cash,
Among numerous toys, you can choose.

Winter

Chinese Papier-mâché

Chinese papier-mâché made of color paper, thin bamboo strips, wires and cotton, is a kind of toy in the shapes of figures, animals, and buildings. On festivals like Lunar New Year's Eve, the Lantern Festival and Mid-Autumn Festival, papier-mâché is considered essential decorations in some areas of Fujian.

Theatrical figures, Chinese papier-mâché,
Putian, Fujian

Paper pumpkin, Sichuan

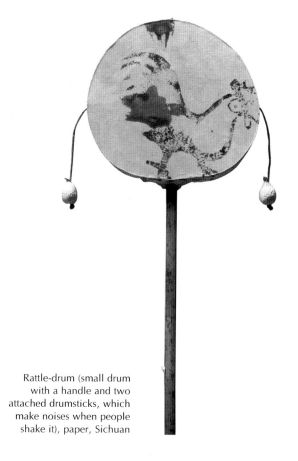

Rattle-drum (small drum with a handle and two attached drumsticks, which make noises when people shake it), paper, Sichuan

General, Chinese papier-mâché,
Hui'an, Fujian

Man and woman generals, characters from a local opera,
Chinese papier-mâché, Hui'an, Fujian

Characters from a local opera, Chinese papier-mâché, Fuzhou, Fujian

Clay Toys from Fengxiang

There are always all sorts of colorful clay toys for sale at the annual temple fair in Fengxiang, Shaanxi, such as lions, tigers, horses, divine cows and auspicious sheep. Devout believers attending the fair will buy several to bring home, to pray for safety and happiness.

Large squatting tiger, clay, Fengxiang, Shaanxi

Squatting tiger, clay, Xifeng, Gansu

Large Squatting Tiger

Large squatting tiger is exemplary of Fengxiang's clay sculpture. Large in size and colorful, it looks powerful and majestic. In the old days, tiger was believed to be able to keep away evil spirits and disaster. Even today this type of toy is still popular among the folk and is sold on occasions of festivals. The body of the Large squatting tiger is made of clay. When it is dried, it is coated in white; then auspicious designs like peony, pomegranate, "Buddha's hand", or calabash are drawn on its body, and followed by bright colors. It is decorative, giving an impression of dynamics and festivity.

Tiger

The tiger is a symbol of auspiciousness, and therefore very popular with people. Many things related to children are decorated with tiger skin designs. People used to buy their children clay tiger whistles at markets during festivals hoping that would bring fortune and safety to children.

Black tiger, clay, made by Gu Biao and Ding Guo'an, Wuxi, Jiangsu

Clay tiger whistles, Niejiazhuang Village, Gaomi, Shandong

Large hanging tiger, clay, Fengxiang, Shaanxi

Clay Hanging Tiger

Clay hanging tigers were also believed to be able to protect families from evil spirits. The material of the toy is
clay combined with pulp, covered with a layer of lacquer
polish. The toy is in fact a large head of a tiger. People
paint designs of pomegranate, peony and lotus on the face
of the tiger to make it more colorful and awe-inspiring.

Two rabbits, clay, Fengxiang, Shaanxi

Horse with a red saddle, clay,
Fengxiang, Shaanxi

Flour Dough Sculpture

The material of dough sculpture is flour, so it is popular among China's northern areas that produce wheat. This type of toy has a big variety, including ancient and modern figures, birds and beasts, flowers, fish and insects, etc. Some are painted with colors after soaking, while others are kneaded with colors, and some decorated with Chinese dates and beans.

Legendary figure, dough sculpture, Guanxian County, Shandong

Three skilled women, dough sculpture,
Yangcheng, Shanxi

Tiger, dough sculpture, Shanxi

Theatrical figures, dough sculpture,
Yangcheng, Shanxi

Doll on a horse, dough sculpture, Shanxi

Dolls, dough sculpture, Guanxian County, Shandong

Flowered tigers, dough sculpture, Shanxi

Ceramic Whistles of Jianshui, Yunnan

Jianshui County of Yunnan is renowned for producing ceramics. The ceramic toys are a favorite. The toys are largely whistles in concise but vivid shapes of all kinds of animals, as well as small objects for children to play and use. The sand clay roughcast is thinly glazed, and then fired. The glaze is greenish yellow, with a little brown, giving it a simple and antique charm.

Monkey riding a horse, ceramic whistle, Jianshui, Yunnan

Kettle, ceramic whistle, Jianshui, Yunnan

Pomegranate and peach-shaped pot, ceramic whistle, Jianshui, Yunnan

Riding a bird, ceramic whistle, Jianshui, Yunnan

Ceramic Whistles of Yazhou, Guizhou

Yazhou of Guizhou is teeming with ceramic toys. Potters make small ceramic toys during their spare time, giving them to customers as a gift when selling ceramic products. The majority of these toys are ceramic whistles in the shapes of animals, lifelike and vivid.

Owl, ceramic whistle,
Yazhou, Guizhou

Winter

Dogs, ceramic whistle, Guizhou

Deer, ceramic whistle,
Yazhou, Guizhou

Ox-head pot, ceramic whistle,
Yazhou, Guizhou

Clay Figures of Huishan, Wuxi

Clay figures of Huishan were popular among the Chinese during the 17th to 19th centuries. The most outstanding type of Huishan's clay figure is "Big Afu."

Performer, Wuxi Clay Figure Factory, Jiangsu

Barber, Wuxi Clay Figure Factory, Jiangsu

Selling puppets, Wuxi Clay Figure Factory, Jiangsu

Trades in Old Beijing

These clay toys vividly reproduce a market scene in old Beijing. The carriage driver holds a whip, and in his carriage sits a woman going to visit her parents. The barber shoulders his tools and holds a percussion instrument, the sounds signaling his arrival seem just by your ear; from the distance. The shouts of the goldfish seller and the gongs of the monkey almost reach the ear.

Carriage driver, clay, made by Han Zengqi, Beijing

Goldfish seller, clay, made by Han Zengqi, Beijing

Barber, Wuxi Clay Figure Factory, Jiangsu

Zhang Clay Figurine Master of Tianjin

The colorful clay figurines by masters of the Zhang family have formed a brand. The main themes are human figures, like historical figures and theatrical characters. The masters of the Zhang family emphasize portrayal of expressions on the figures. With bright colors, the lifelike sculptures are of high artistic value, thereby very popular among people.

122

Sisters, made by Fu Changsheng, Tianjin Zhang Clay Figurine Master Workshop

Little girl, made by Yang Zhizhong, Tianjin Zhang Clay Figurine Master Workshop

Playing the zither, made by Wang Runcai,
Tianjin Zhang Clay Figurine Master Workshop

"Blowing up a balloon",
made by Yang Zhizhong,
Tianjin Zhang Clay Figurine
Master Workshop

Winter

Playing *Weiqi* (Go), made by Wang Runcai, Tianjin Zhang Clay
Figurine Master Workshop

Carefree old man, made by Zhang Yusheng, Tianjin Zhang
Clay Figurine Master Workshop

Girl, clay, Niejiazhuang Village,
Gaomi, Shandong

Farmer, clay, Huaiyang,
Henan

Others
Horse and Carriage

Cart with two birds, wood, Tancheng, Shandong

Row of horses, wood, made by Tang Qiliang, Beijing

Horse and carriage, cloth and wood,
made by Tang Qiliang, Beijing

Colorful carriage, wood, Tancheng, Shandong

Flowered Club

Flowered clubs are wooden toys made of willow or poplar wood by using a lathe. The head of the club is hollow, filled inside with sand or beans. Before the wood club head is dried, the handle is stuffed into it; then, some colorful patterns are drawn on it. After it is dried, it will rattle when shaken.

Flowered club, wood,
Tancheng, Shandong

Club with beast mask, wood,
Tancheng, Shandong

Club Figurine

There are two types of club figurines, one is tall and thin, the other is squat and plump. A wooden column body and a round head make up the figurine. It has no arms and legs, for the convenience of children to hold it. The method to make it is, first cutting out the body and head on a lathe, soaking the body in water, then plugging the dried head into the body. When the body is dried, the head, which can shake, will not fall off. Finally eyebrows, eyes and colorful patterns are drawn on it.

Squat club figurines, wood,
Tancheng, Shandong

Tall club figurines, wood,
Tancheng, Shandong

Hemp-stalk Bird

Hemp-stalk birds are another unique toy of Beijing. Different bird shapes are cut out of hemp-stalk cores, with feathers and eyes drawn on them. The legs are made of jujube tree crotches. When the stalk is shaken, the ring hanging at the neck and tail will make the hemp bird nod, resembling a real bird.

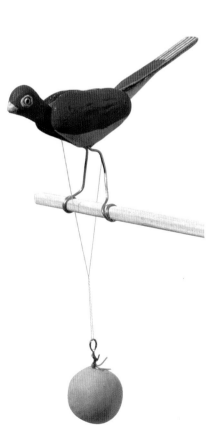

Hemp-stalk bird, made by
Dai Sheng, Beijing

Hemp-stalk bird, made by Zhou
Chongshan, Beijing

图书在版编目（CIP）数据

民间玩具：英文 / 李友友编著 .

—北京：外文出版社，2008

（中国民间文化遗产）

ISBN 978-7-119-04674-7

I . 民… II . 李… III . 玩具—民间工艺—中国—英文 IV.J529

中国版本图书馆 CIP 数据核字（2008）第 090541 号

出版策划：李振国
英文翻译：冯　鑫
英文审定：May Yee　　王明杰
责任编辑：杨春燕
文案编辑：蔡跃蕾　　刘芳念
装帧设计：黎　红
印刷监制：韩少乙

本书由中国轻工业出版社授权出版

民间玩具

李友友　编著

© 2008 外文出版社

出版发行：

外文出版社出版（中国北京百万庄大街 24 号）

邮政编码：100037

网　　　址：www.flp.com.cn

电　　　话：008610-68320579（总编室）

　　　　　　008610-68995852（发行部）

　　　　　　008610-68327750（版权部）

制　　版：

北京维诺传媒文化有限公司

印　　刷：

北京外文印刷厂

开　　本：787mm×1092mm　　1/16　印张：8.75

2008 年第 1 版第 1 次印刷

（英）

ISBN 978-7-119-04674-7

09800（平）

85-E-646 P